IMAGES OF ENGLAND

ERDINGTON
VOLUME II

IMAGES OF ENGLAND

ERDINGTON
VOLUME II

PETER DRAKE AND MARIAN BAXTER

TEMPUS

Frontispiece: Johnson Road decorated for the coronation, photographed on 2 June 1953.

First published 2003

Tempus Publishing Limited
The Mill, Brimscombe Port,
Stroud, Gloucestershire, GL5 2QG

British Library Cataloguing in Publication Data.
A catalogue record for this book is available from the British Library.

ISBN 0 7524 3057 2

Typesetting and origination by Tempus Publishing Limited
Printed in Great Britain by Midway Colour Print, Wiltshire

Contents

Yenton Bowls Club pictured just before the war. George Booth is second from the right on the front row.

Introduction

What do today's residents think of the look of the modern Erdington? The compilers would hazard a guess that the following might give a flavour of how the area is currently viewed. A pretty mixed suburb with a decidedly posh part close to Wylde Green and also some distinctly dodgy estates, no names. A suburb rather like the city centre, where old and attractive buildings have routinely been pulled down since the war to be replaced by some pretty charmless buildings. Despite the investment in the High Street it lacks a character of its own and is dominated by the pound shops. The Green and the Six Ways at each end of the High Street lack the charm shown in old photographs. The frequency of the cross-city trains, traffic congestion from the Six Ways to Gravelly Hill and the vagaries of the buses dominate the thinking of those commuters who live in Erdington. Secondary schooling in the district and the desire to get their children into Sutton schools influence the house buying decisions of Erdington parents.

How tempting it is to look back to another time and another century. Contrast the perception above with this description of Erdington in 1850. It is taken from the reminiscences of an old Erdington resident and his view of the district when he was a child. He wrote:

> As to Erdington village itself, it was a struggling hamlet given to agricultural pursuits, with a shop here and there grouped around the parish church. Between a point near the church and the Swan Inn there were fields attached to neighbouring farms, with scarcely a house the greater part of the way, bordered by hedgerows and ditches, an occasional tree or old barn breaking the monotony of the scene.
>
> The railway had not been cut, and the only means of public conveyance between the hamlet and Birmingham was an old bus which made the journey between New Street, Birmingham and Sutton two or three times a day. A road toll had to be paid at the bottom of Gravelly Hill … The roads were none too well kept and were under the control of the Surveyor of Highways, who was appointed by the vestry meeting.

The Erdington Workhouse was an old ramshackle building, standing opposite the Village Green on the spot now occupied by the Carnegie Free Library, at the top of Mason Road and the adjoining premises of the London City and Midland Bank.

The railway was not constructed until 1861, and even at so late a period as this the Tame was a river in which trout rose to the May fly, and in which many varieties of fish afforded ample sport for anglers, both young and old, who frequented its banks below Bromford Bridge.

The constabulary arrangements were in the hands of the Watching and Light Board. This authority had the services of one constable, a man named John Pearson. For many years he bore the responsibility of policemanship upon his shoulders, and he was several times rather knocked about by the roughs who came poaching in Erdington. The lock-up and magistrates court was in Bell Lane, the thoroughfare now known as Orphanage Road, and when a prisoner was committed to gaol Pearson had to convey the offender from here to the county gaol at Warwick. On one occasion when he was conveying several men they overpowered him in the train, nearly killed him and made good their escape. After this a second officer was sworn in.

The scale of change in the one hundred and fifty years since these reminiscences would have been quite amazing to Erdington's Victorian residents. In the pages that follow are the photographs we have chosen to chart the development of Erdington from the 1850s hamlet portrayed above to the modern suburb. Whether it is all progress is a matter of personal preference but hopefully this book will inform that debate and evoke more than a few memories.

Acknowledgements

The compilers would like to thank the following for their help: Andrew Maxam, David Harvey, Roger Carpenter, Patrick Hayes, Mr and Mrs Revill, the members of the Erdington Historical Society, the staff of Local Studies and History Section of Birmingham Reference Library for the use of their collection of photographs, and all the readers of our earlier volume of Erdington photographs. Unless otherwise stated all the photographs reproduced here are held in the Local Studies Library. Special thanks to Brian Hall for proofreading part of the text.

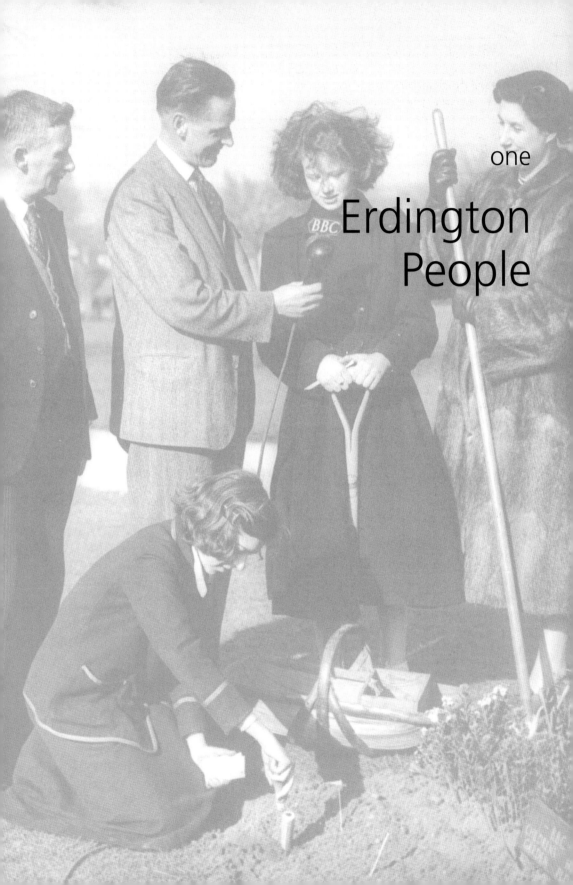

one

Erdington
People

Left: Tom Green was Erdington's first appointed postman. Isaac James kept a grocer's shop next to the Swan Inn, he employed an Isaac Carter who acted as postman for which he received 2d per letter for delivery. This was paid in addition to postage dues. In 1874 Thomas Green commenced his duties and in 1878 was officially appointed postman, with Carter acting as auxiliary. According to A.H. Saxton in his book *Bygone Erdington* Tom Green was eighty-one years of age in June 1928. Unfortunately he was burned to death in September 1928.

Below: Laying the foundation stone at Jaffray Road Hospital, 1884. The Jaffray Hospital, standing in eight acres of grounds, was built by John Jaffray and was opened by the Prince of Wales (later Edward VIII) on 29 November 1885 as a place where the helpless would be properly looked after and brought back to health.

Opposite above: Mr Henry Fowler's farmyard, Holifast, Erdington, 1893. Holifast Grange stood in Chester Road and was an eighteenth-century red brick-built house with a Doric porch.

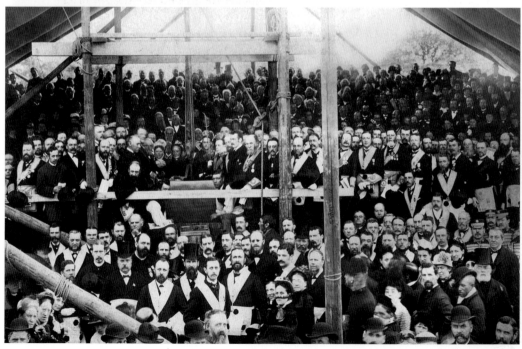

Below: Entrance to Pype Hayes Park, at the point of divergence of the later and ancient Chester Road, 1894. Pype Hayes Hall and Park were purchased by Birmingham City Council in 1919 for £10,000. The Park was officially opened on 24 March 1920. Pre-Roman, Chester Road is one of the oldest roads in the area. In 1759 the Chester Road Turnpike Act set charges of 1d for a pack-horse or mule and 3d for a horse and cart to use the road.

Above: Mr F.B. Collier & Sons. The business was founded by F.B. Collier in 1858, when he opened his first shop, a chemist, in Orphanage Road. In October 1866 he moved into purpose-built premises on the High Street, near to the old Public Hall. The chemist shop included a grocery. The 'Yellow Shop', as it became known, was run by Mr Collier's two sons and was well known throughout the area.

Opposite below: Jaffray Road Hospital grounds. Members of the Six Ways Baptist Church celebrate the end of the Boer War.

Right: Thomas Barnsley, one of the Trustees of the Josiah Mason Orphanage. According to Sir Josiah Mason's wishes the trustees had to be laymen, Protestants and living within ten miles of the orphanage. Sir J. Benjamin Stone took this photograph in 1908.

Below: Visitors at the Grange. The Stone family pose for a formal photograph, taken by Sir J. Benjamin Stone (front row) with their visitors Joseph and Tom Semmer (on the right in the back row) from New Orleans. The photograph is taken outside The Grange, which today is the Taylor Hospice in Grange Road.

Children, girls only, in the classroom at the Josiah Mason Orphanage, photographed by J. Benjamin Stone in 1908. The orphanage fronted Bell Lane (Orphanage Road) and opened in 1869. It survived as an orphanage and later a school, open to day-pupils, until it was demolished in 1963.

Children, boys only, in the classroom at Josiah Mason Orphanage. Photographed by J. Benjamin Stone in 1908. Josiah Mason was born in Kidderminster in 1795. He was the epitome of the Victorian entrepreneur and philanthropist, using the wealth from his successful pen-making business to fund the orphanage. He died in 1881.

A popular figure in Erdington, William Nock was born in Derby in 1826. He moved to Birmingham in 1851, married in 1852 and arrived in Erdington in 1875 after a successful career as a master builder in Lozells. In Erdington he took over a large brickfield in Holly Lane. The brick works had opened in the early 1860s but it was not until Mr Nock took over that more bricks were made in one day than were made in one week at the turn of the century. Many of Erdington's houses are built with the firm's bricks, and over twenty million bricks from this company were used in the construction of Fort Dunlop. In 1890 William became an overseer for Aston and was awarded the honorary title of J.P. The brick works closed in 1965 after the last of the clay had been extracted.

Officers of the Sutton Coldfield Company Volunteers at The Grange, 27 July 1901. Photographed by J. Benjamin Stone.

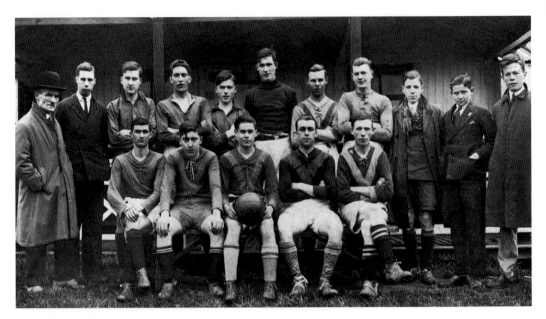

Erdington Congregational Football Club, 1930/31.

Erdington versus Leicester hockey match, 1898.

A Henry Cotton golf exhibition. Henry Cotton drives off before an interested gallery at Pype Hayes golf course.

Pype Hayes golf course. J.M. Cawsey, the professional golfer at Pype Hayes Golf Club, gives instruction to young future champions, 28 May 1953.

Transport Garage, Tyburn Road. Long-serving garage engineers on a one-day token strike, 10 March 1961. In a dispute about wages and a bonus scheme the Tyburn Road garage was the main repair works for the Corporation's bus fleet.

Percy Thrower, of the BBC asks a question of Joan Bradley, of Hillyfields Road, Erdington, on a visit to the *Children's Hour* gardening plot at Rookery Park. While Wendy Folger prepares the ground for gladioli planting, Miss Peggy Bacon, *Children's Hour* organiser (Midland Region), holds the hoe. Park keeper, Mr L.O. Cooper, is an interested spectator. This event took place during a broadcast of the *Children's Hour* feature 'Our garden from Rookery Park' on 21 April 1953.

Patrick Hayes. Patrick describes himself as an Irish Brummie living and working in Birmingham. Son of a Royal Navy officer and a farmer's daughter from County Galway, he was educated at St Philip's grammar school and obtained a degree in Drama at the University of London. At present Patrick works as a Community Arts Worker, is the author of local history books, writes short stories, plays and television scripts. He has worked together with author Marian Baxter on several projects over the years including the production of a play and video on the murder of Mary Ashford. A man of many talents, including the study of Spanish and French in which he tutors for Adult Education, Patrick even found time to marry in 2003.
(Gary Price)

Horse-drawn fire engine, 1901.

A rick fire at the farmyard on the corner of Chester Road and Grange Lane, 31 July 1899. The local fire engine is in attendance.

two

Mainly
Trams

THE 616 E

Above: Tram 650 on the number 2 route on the High Street approaching the Six Ways. The High Street was so narrow that for part of the way single track working was necessary. It was only 39ft wide with a carriageway of 25ft – far too restricted for double working.

Opposite: Two views of trams on the High Street, the top one taken on 16 April 1929 and the bottom one in May 1938. The Erdington Tramways Act of 1902 granted permission for the district to build a tramway route to the city. This met local opposition. Meetings were held and feelings ran very high against the idea. Eventually a poll was demanded by the opposing ratepayers and they won the day. The tramway would lead from the High Street past the Six Ways to link up with the existing route and tracks at Gravelly Hill. Trams began running the route on 22 April 1907. The total cost of the construction and the equipment was £35,790.

Above and below: Two views of traffic at the Six Ways showing alterations to the island. The top photograph is dated 29 September 1938. Both views are taken from Gravelly Hill North with the High Street on the right.

Outside the Post Office on the Sutton New Road on the day of the official opening of the bypass, 21 October 1938.

A photograph taken further along the Sutton New Road on the day it was opened by the Lord Mayor of Birmingham, Alderman E.R. Canning. Trams had been allowed to run along the central carriageway for several weeks in advance of the opening, taking the pressure off the High Street.

Above and below: Two further views of Slade Road trams. The top view is of tramcar number 314 starting its journey from Stockland Green to Steelhouse Lane in the city centre. The lower postcard view shows a tramcar passing George Road and approaching Adams and Hodgkinson's grocery stores at No. 164 Slade Lane.

Short Heath and Steelhouse Lane tramcars passing under the LNWR railway bridge in Slade Road. The bridge was a notorious black spot for accidents, pedestrians only having a metal rail on one side as protection. The footpaths were widened when buses took over from trams on the route in 1953, and traffic lights introduced, but the dangers were not finally removed until a separate pedestrian bridge was cut and opened on 29 October 1957.

Tramcar number 719 on the 78 route from Short Heath passing the prefabs.

Tyburn Road tram tracks photographed on 21 January 1952, just a year before the trams finally departed from the city.

Tramcar number 706 on the 79 route travelling on the Lichfield Road close to Cuckoo Road bridge with Salford Park on its left.

Above and below: Two postcard views of the Chester Road tram terminus at Wylde Green. The postcards come from the Meachem collection of postcards presented to the Central Library by Norman Meachem, a local Erdington historian. The views date from the 1920s.

Tramcar number 616 at Erdington tram terminus on the last day of running, 4 July 1953. The last tram is apparently being driven by the Chairman of the Transport Committee Alderman Harry Watton.

PROPOSED STEAM TRAMWAY EXTENSION

ASTON TO CHESTER ROAD.

OBJECTIONS:—

1.—That they will **monopolize the Roads** with unsightly **STEAM ENGINES** and cars, and cause considerable danger and inconvenience to the vehicular traffic, for which the Roads were made.

2.—That the Railway and Omnibus Companies have hitherto provided adequate accommodation for the district unattended by danger, and will naturally meet any increased want.

3.—That the Tram Roads will have to be Lighted, Guttered, and Kerbed, which will **involve an extra rate** in the Hamlet. and only benefit the few.

4.—That the **speed of the STEAM ENGINES,** combined with the unavoidable noise and rattle, will frighten the horses, and endanger foot passengers—especially children—crossing the Roads.

5.—That they will increase **Sunday Traffic** along the Roads.

6.—That it is not solely a question for carriage owners but the privacy of Residences fronting the Tram Roads **will be overlooked** and their value depreciated, and the present rural aspect of the district, which has attracted many to reside in the locality, will be destroyed.

7.—That they are not promoted by anyone having any interest in the neighbourhood beyond **speculation.**

RATEPAYERS OF ERDINGTON.

A Poll has been demanded on the above question, and will take place between the hours of 10 a.m. and 4 p.m. on **TUESDAY, DECEMBER the 4th,** at the Public Hall. **VOTE EARLY,** and crush the "**MONSTER**" by an overwhelming majority.

From Saxton's *Bygone Erdington.*

Erdington railway station. 1862 saw the opening of the line to Sutton. Two companies proposing different routes from the city centre to Sutton bid for the franchise to build the line. If the other bid had been successful, instead of the familiar locations of stations, the line would have left New Street via Saltley and crossed to Gravelly Hill by the Tyburn Road. It would then have climbed past Wood End to a station in Mason Road and on to another station by the Orphanage, now Yenton School, before travelling to Maney. A great feat of engineering but resented by some locals.

An early postcard view of Gravelly Hill station. This particular card was posted on 17 March 1905. In 1900 the *Railway Magazine* reported of the Sutton line 'the service is so good that it is not uncommon for those who reside on the branch and have their business in the city to go to and fro for their meals'. The likelihood of an Erdington commuter popping home for lunch and then back to work in the city centre nowadays is not high! In 1929 Erdington had twenty-five up and twenty-seven down trains doing the journey to the city centre in fifteen minutes.

three

Garages and Petrol Stations

Above and below: Two views of the very attractive looking Goosemoor Lane garage in May 1950. A fine suburban house, a sunny day, splendid cars in the garage – not exactly today's functional petrol station-cum–small-scale-supermarket.

Sotherns service garage on the corner of Slade Road with Victoria Road in November 1928. A model T Ford stops to fill up on the forecourt.

Sand Pits garage in Slade Road on 24 March 1952. An Austin and a Standard Flying 16 are parked up.

The garage becomes more functional. Slade Road service station on 10 August 1959 playing host to two Morris Minors, a Vauxhall 14 or 16, a Ford Prefect 100E and, peeping its nose out under the Mobil sign, a Bedford CA van.

An unlikely setting for a second-hand car business, Ideal Motors, 'used car specialists', in Coton Lane. Photographed in August 1935.

An unofficial garage-cum-workshop at No. 112 Summer Road. The City's Planning Department took the photograph as evidence in the planning process.

Wood End garage in Wood End Lane, February 1976.

A very well-respected local garage – Hooks garage in Wood End Road - photographed on 29 September 1959. At the time of writing (spring 2003) the last garage on the site had been demolished and is awaiting redevelopment.

On the opposite side of the road was Glen Fern garage, caught on camera here in June 1976.

Patrick Motors garage on Gravelly Hill North, 18 March 1960. The cars on the forecourt were an Austin A40 Utility Brake, a Rover P4, a Standard Vanguard and an Austin A40 Devon. The garage was subsequently taken over by Kennings.

The Six Ways was ringed with garages. This is the Apex service station at the junction of Summer Road and Sutton New Road. The site is now occupied by an electronics shop.

The same premises but now George Hancox's Ford dealership. It is pictured here on 6 May 1960. The whole development here is currently awaiting demolition after a fire.

Opposite above: Opposite Harry Parkes sports shop on Gravelly Hill North was Bateman's garage, seen here on 18 April 1956.

Opposite below: Chamber's car showrooms next to the Queens Head and Greens at the Six Ways. The photograph shows part of the Highcroft Hall carnival procession in August 1957.

Above and below: Two views of Abbey garage, virtually opposite the Abbey on Sutton Road. The top photograph is from 21 June 1954 and in the showrooms are a Rover 60, an Austin A40 Somerset, an MG Midget and Armstrong-Siddeley Sapphire. A Standard Vanguard Estate is parked off the road. The lower photograph, taken a few years later on 10 May 1967, shows the garage offering a Morris 1100 and Minis.

Bradley's garage on Gravelly Lane, 26 November 1951. The site is now a garden centre. Among the cars in for attention are a Morris van, an Austin Cambridge, an Austin A70 Hampshire, a Triumph Renown and a Sunbeam Talbot 90.

Yenton garage at Wylde Green on 26 July 1955. The site has seen several new garages and changes of ownership since this photograph was taken and in fact a new garage has just opened. A selection of Austins can be seen on the forecourt along with a Wrensons van parked by the two pedestrians on the right.

A lorry comes to a halt in the flower beds outside Yenton garage on 22 March 1960.

Jack Harper's driving school at No. 39 Sutton Road on 10 May 1967.

Marsh Hill service station in 2003. A classic example of a charmless building and a far cry from the Goosemoor Lane garage at the beginning of the chapter. It has now closed.

SP car showroom at 54–56 Station Road, Erdington, in December 1971.

A postcard view from around 1955 of the Six Ways showing Abbey Garage on the High Street shortly after it had been taken over from Jones Brothers. The building had a Belfast roof and after one heavy fall of snow collapsed, damaging several cars. The premises were sold to make way for Marley Building Products DIY business. The premises were large, with the garage capable of holding 150 cars.

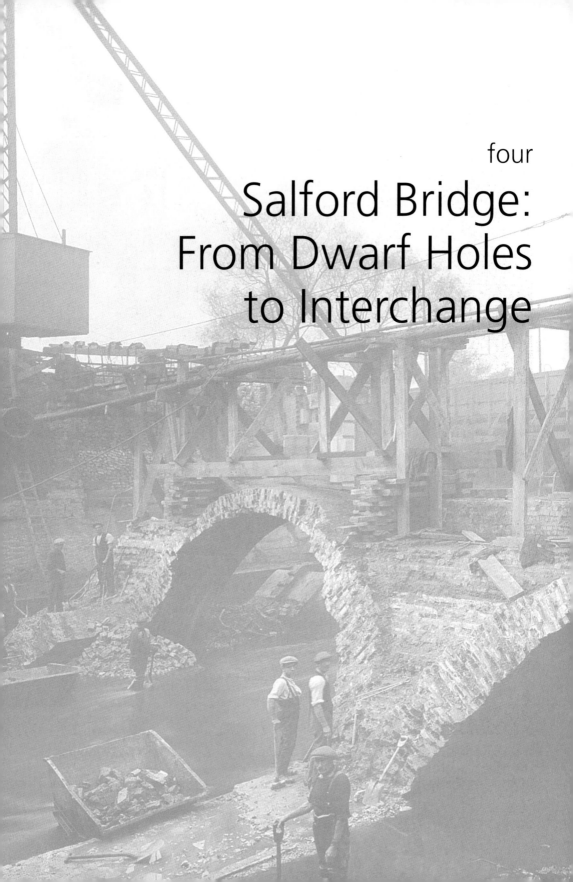

four

Salford Bridge:
From Dwarf Holes
to Interchange

Dwarf Holes at Gravelly Hill, *c.* 1895. According to Erdington local historian, N.C. Meachem, these caves had a strong claim to Stone Age connections. They consisted of two or more holes carved out of the sandstone and gave access to large artificial ones. A third hole used to lie below the level of the canal towpath, which was built up to cover it in 1840. A deed of 1490 refers to several parcels of land including two crofts of land called Dwarffenholes. Unfortunately they were destroyed when Spaghetti was built in 1973, so we shall never know their true origins.

Salford Bridge, September 1922. The ancient ford and bridge were some fifty yards upstream. Originally there may have been a narrow footbridge, and the carts would have used the shallow ford alongside. A bridge on the present site was first mentioned in 1290 in a lawsuit brought by Thomas de Maindenhache against William de Bermingham, concerning the fishing rights at 'Scrafford Bridge' as it was then called. It probably derived from the old English 'scroef' meaning a cave, hollow or pit, and referred to the hollows or caves in the sandstone cliff nearby.

Salford Bridge, January 1924. It is interesting to see how the present name was derived from the ancient versions. The 'Scrafford' form persists throughout the fourteenth century but with different spellings such as 'Schrafford Bruggee' in 1309 and ten years later 'Schrafforde Bridge'. In an account by Leland in 1540, describing his journey from Birmingham to the 'Southeton', he states that a mile past 'Bremischum' he passed over 'Sharforf Bridge'. Since then the name has varied from Shrawford Bridge in 1596, to Stafford Bridge in 1793.

Salford Bridge, August 1924. Salford Bridge was eventually derived from 'Safford Bridge' shown on a map of Erdington in 1760. Salford Bridge is shown on Smith's Map of Warwickshire 1804 and 1818, and in Kelly's Directory in 1867.

Salford Bridge, September 1924. In 1810 a new iron bridge was built, which was widened and lengthened in around 1840 when the new canal was cut. On the left parapet two stones were inscribed: 'This bridge replaces two old bridges, which had a width of 36ft between the parapet walls. The southernmost bridge, which consisted of three brick arches, carried the highway over the River Tame and was erected a few yards east of the ancient ford known as 'Schrafford' or 'Scraford'. It was erected in the year 1810, and widened around 1845 when the canal was made and the other bridge of cast iron constructed over it. Records refer to an earlier bridge over the river in the year 1290'.

Salford Bridge, September 1924. Sir Arthur Steel Maitland, Minister of Labour and Member of Parliament for Erdington, opened this new bridge in October 1926. It was begun three years earlier as part of the unemployment relief programme. The older bridge was about a century old when it was replaced, but the other bridges existed here for seven centuries and before that there was a ford across the River Tame, some fifty yards upstream.

Salford Bridge, October 1925.

Salford Bridge. This photograph shows the old bridge over the canal.

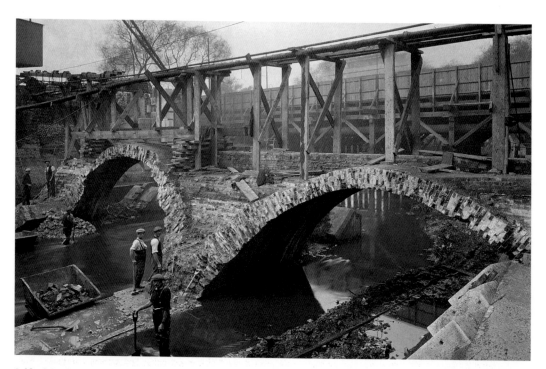

Salford Bridge, April 1925. The following few photographs show the demolition of the old bridge and the building of the new one.

Salford Bridge. The architect's designs for the Salford bridge reconstruction. The bridge was changed to its present style in 1926. It cost £100,000 and took three years to build. Sir Arthur Steel Maitland opened it on 13 October 1926.

Salford Bridge, September 1926. The Lord Mayor, who presided at the opening ceremony, described the bridge as one of the greatest public improvements in the city. The building gave work to 2,300 unemployed people every week over the whole period. In 1955, eight traffic lights were installed at the junction of Gravelly Hill and Tyburn Road relieving the police of one of their biggest traffic headaches outside of the city centre.

Salford Bridge. This photograph of Salford Bridge by Errol Francis is taken from a portfolio of images of the city compiled by him for the exhibition 'Birmingham: The Architecture of Two Ecologies' held in Birmingham Central Library in 1999. Other equally interesting images from the exhibition are available in the Local Studies section of the Central Library. Errol has recently worked as artist in residence at the old All Saints Hospital in Winson Green.

A wonderful view looking towards the old Salford Bridge, taken in September 1922.

Salford Bridge, 1924. The old Salford Bridge with the number 2 tram and Birmingham to Streetly bus passing over it.

Salford Bridge, 1925. The corner of Tyburn Road and Gravelly Hill.

The Lichfield Road at Salford Bridge, April 1928. Salford Lake is on the left and the flat ground in front of the lake now homes the Power League five-a-side football site.

Salford Bridge. The new bridge stands on the right and Money & Bostridge's tobacco shop on the corner of Leamington road is on the left. This was one of the oldest tobacconists in Erdington and the sellers of the series of these three cards.

Salford Sports Stadium, 1951. The running and cycle track at Salford Park were estimated to cost £12,000, and was an interim stage towards the provision of a municipal sports stadium. The track had a 2ft ash running track (41/2 laps to the mile surrounded by a 22ft cycle track (4 laps to the mile) with a minimum banking of 6ft and ends were surfaced with non-skid asphalt. The architects were Harry W. Wheedon and Partners.

Salford Park. In this view of Salford Pool the old pumping station chimney can be seen on the left and Copeley Hill on the right.

Salford Park, Gravelly Hill, Birmingham

Above: Salford Park, looking towards the nut and screw works in Leamington Road, *c.* 1928. This, with certain adjoining lands was originally known as Aston Reservoir. Used by Birmingham Water Works it became redundant and was leased to White City (Birmingham) Limited in 1914 to provide an exhibition ground and amusement park. The lease was terminated on 31 March 1917 and in 1919 part of the land and reservoirs was leased to the Parks Department as a public park. The forty-three acre park was officially opened on 6 December 1919.

Opposite above: Salford Park being prepared for the construction of the Gravelly Hill Interchange, August 1968. The scheme to link the M1, M5 and M6 motorways was launched in 1958 when the minister of transport and Civil Aviation commissioned Sir Owen Williams and Partners, consulting engineers, to carry out studies for a new route. There were two possibilities for the route. A peripheral route around the Birmingham conurbation, or a more direct route through the conurbation. As the majority of the traffic had destinations in the conurbation, the closer the Links could be brought into the centre of Birmingham the better. Work began on the first sections of the Midland Links Motorways in 1964. The Link Motorway was to include the M6 and the M5.

Opposite below: Gravelly Hill Interchange, October 1969. A Save the Fish campaign helped protect 250,000 fish, which were temporarily moved from Salford Pool during construction, the largest of which was a twenty-pound carp. Spaghetti Junction appears in the *Guinness Book of Records* as 'the most complex interchange on the British road system'.

Above: Gravelly Hill Interchange, September 1969. The Midlands Links scheme consists of sixty-six miles of three-lane motorway. The link between the M5 and the M6 was achieved in May 1970. The length includes the multi-level Gravelly Hill Interchange and when it was built it was the largest of its kind in Europe. The brochure for the official opening ceremony of the Interchange states 'this interchange provides a free flow motorway link, via Birmingham City Council's Aston Expressway, into the centre of the city and also connects with the A38 and other local roads'.

Opposite above: Spaghetti Junction starts to take shape, September 1970. The last link of the M6 to be built was the length between the junctions with the A34 Walsall Road at Great Barr and the Newport Road at Castle Bromwich. From Great Barr the route proceeds to Gravelly Hill, through residential and industrial areas. The motorway then continues through Gravelly Hill on viaducts over canals, railways and sewage works, and alongside the then old Birmingham racecourse to Castle Bromwich.

Opposite below: Gravelly Hill Interchange, May 1971. A total of fifteen years were spent in the planning and construction of Spaghetti Junction. Work started in 1968 and took four years to complete, at a cost of £10.8 million to build. In today's prices (2003) that is equivalent to £86.2 million. The original construction of Spaghetti Junction involved 13,000 tonnes of steel reinforcement and 134,000cm (175,000 cubic yards) of concrete.

Gravelly Hill Interchange, May 1971. Although the interchange only covers 0.06 miles of the M6 motorway, there is an additional 2.5 miles of slip roads. The opening of Salford Interchange (Spaghetti Junction) on 24 May 1972 by the Right Honourable Peter Walker, MBE, MP, meant that a continuous 304 miles of motorway was available from just north of Carlisle to London.

Gravelly Hill Interchange, May 1972. During the first year of opening the average flow of vehicles was 40,000 per day. This has increased to over 140,000 vehicles per day. Since 1972, an estimated 1.25 billion vehicles have passed through the complex, and approximately 5 million tonnes of freight passes through the interchange every week.

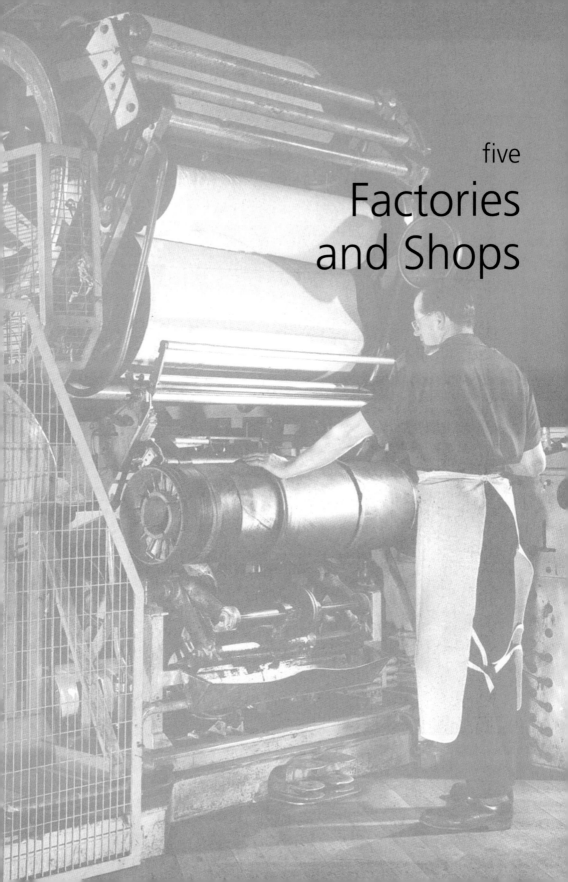

five

Factories
and Shops

An aerial view of the Dunlop Works, Tyburn Road. In July 1919 the famous tyre factory was little more than a cottage situated in Holly Lane. It was John Dunlop, a veterinary surgeon, born in Scotland, who developed the pneumatic tyre for his son's tricycle. The Dunlop factory was developed in Erdington because below the fields was an inexhaustible supply of water, and large quantities were needed in the manufacturing process.

An aerial view of the Dunlop Works near to the Chester Road railway bridge, 15 October 1937. Development was rapid. By 1938, when they were celebrating fifty years of growth, the massive commercial block dominated the Birmingham skyline and a worldwide network of companies had been set up.

Above: Fort Dunlop. In the 1960s the Erdington factory was the largest of its 110 plants and the biggest tyre-making plant in the British Commonwealth. It employed 10,000 of its 100,000 employees. The Fort covered nearly 300 acres, had well over 3 million square feet of factory area and nearly five miles of railway sidings and marshalling yards, a network of wide roads and a heliport.

Right: One of the car tyre building machines at Fort Dunlop. Rubber for the tyre production used to arrive from the 80,000-acre plantations Dunlop owned in Malaya.

DUNLOP TYRES

AS BRITISH AS THE FLAG

DUNLOP RUBBER COMPANY LIMITED
Fort Dunlop   BIRMINGHAM
Branches throughout the World.

Left: An advertisement for Dunlop tyres taken from *Birmingham Talks to the World: Activities and Industries of England's Second City,* 1932.

Below: 'Inspecting car tyres at Europe's largest tyre factory at Fort Dunlop'. The inscription on the back of this undated photograph.

Opposite below: Fisher and Ludlow. After the war the firm took the opportunity to transfer their main body construction business to the former Vickers Armstrong aircraft factory at Castle Bromwich. The heavy presses were moved to the Castle Bromwich plant and production of the Standard Vanguard body shell was commenced during 1946.

Above: Fisher and Ludlow. Thousands of British cars were fitted with Fisher and Ludlow parts: compressed body panels, chassis parts, valances, brake drums, hubcaps and engine pumps. Second World War work included producing components for barrage balloons, armoured vehicles and amphibious vehicles. Wartime bombings did serious damage to the Fisher and Ludlow factories.

SU Carburettors, Wood End Lane, October 1952. SU Carburettors was established in London in 1910. On 1 October 1926 they were bought by Morris and production was moved to the old part of the Wolseley factory at Adderley Park.

Entrance to SU Carburettors, Wood Lane, October 1952. In 1931 SU developed a petrol pump and also aircraft carburettors. By 1938 they were supplying carburettors to Napier engines which were fitted to Tempest and Typhoon aircraft. In 1942 SU developed fuel-injection pumps, which replaced the aircraft carburettor. During the Second World War the SU factory moved from Adderley Park to Shirley.

Bomb Proof Construction Co., Wood Lane, March 1955.

Birlec made electrical furnaces and were established in 1927 at Birmingham Electrical Furnaces Limited. Birlec was the trade name for furnaces made by BEF. They took over a strip of land beside the Tyburn Road that backed onto the Birmingham and Fazeley Canal and built a factory there. They were particularly successful in the 1930s when electric furnaces were brought to replace other types of furnace. After 1945 they became AEI–Birlec and opened a new site at Aldridge. The Tyburn Road site eventually closed and moved to Aldridge.

Bromford Tube Company Limited, Bromford Lane, 1949. Bromford Tubes was formed in 1921. In the 1930s Stewarts and Lloyds acquired a half interest in Bromford Tubes. In 1972 the company had a capacity of 80,000 tons of seamless tubes from three Pilger mills. Its production included carbon steel tubes and a wide variety of alloy steel tubes. The company served several important industries such as power generation, oil refining and chemical processing where resistance to high temperature, pressure and corrosion was paramount.

Cincinnati, Kingsbury Road. The Cincinnati Milling Machine Company made general purpose milling machines for the shaping of tools. The large wheel which stood next to the Birmingham and Fazeley Canal on the Kingsbury Road, and which one of the authors, as a child, thought belonged to Cincinnati, was in fact erected by George H. Hughes Limited whose premises were in Edgmond Avenue.

Rymond's shop. Mr J.H. Rymond purchased the butcher's shop from Mr Johnson and it was to become the best-known butchers in Erdington. The shop had its own slaughter house at the rear. When he retired, J.H. moved to The Cottage in Church Road and his son, Arthur, took over the business adding a pork butchering establishment to the site. A member of Erdington District Council, J.H. Rymond become an elected member of Birmingham City Council when Erdington was absorbed into the city. He and Alderman Quinney negotiated the purchase of the Canwell Estates for the Corporation.

Erdington Market, June 1929.

The Co-Operative, 230–234 Wheelwright Road, May 1963.

The Co-Operative, Slade Road, December 1963.

Philip Jackson's furniture shop, which stood on the corner of Reservoir Road and Gravelly Hill North at Six Ways, Erdington, June 1960.

The corner of Gravelly Hill North at Six Ways, Erdington, February 1961. The Lunch Box was for many years a popular place for a coffee and a sandwich, but the premises are currently empty after recent closure of the café. The first Birmingham Municipal Bank in Birmingham opened on 1 September 1919. The Birmingham Municipal Bank merged with the TSB in 1976. The Erdington building is now used by the HSBC Bank.

W.M. Taylor & Sons, High Street, around the 1950s. W.H. Taylor & Sons, drapers, started in 1887 in the front room of a house in Potters Hill. William Munton Taylor came to Birmingham to take up a position at Newbury's General Store which stood on the old Lewis's site. To help supplement the family income, Mrs Taylor opened her own little shop in the front room of their house. When Mr Taylor gave up his job rather than sack a member of his staff he joined his wife in the business. The business grew until it became a limited company and branches were opened in Erdington, Kings Heath, Sutton Coldfield and Solihull. The Erdington branch was rebuilt in 1969. In October 1971 the Erdington store was purchased by Owen Owen.

Above: High Street and the corner of New Road, May 1953.

Opposite below: High Street, Erdington, March 1982. Shops in this photograph include J.W. Wassell's shoe shop which advertised footwear for all the family, Barney's, the walk around clothing store and Freedom Travel, the holiday company which went into liquidation in a blaze of publicity. This photograph taken in 1982 also shows the two-way traffic. The traffic today, in this section of the road, is one-way only.

Orphanage Road Stores in October 1957.

Orphanage Road, July 1961. The building to the left is the Labour Party headquarters, John Bates & Sons was a building firm, while to the right is Mitchell's and Butler's off-licence.

six

Pubs

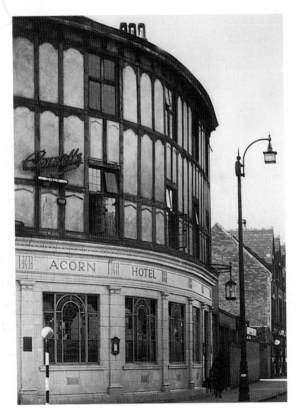

The Acorn at 196 High Street on the corner with Church Road opposite Burton's, in around 1938. The top storey of the Acorn was later removed at the beginning of the fifties as it had fallen into disuse before the block was demolished in 1973, and the existing Acorn, without the style, was built.

A rather romantic view of the Green Man opposite St Barnabas church. The Acorn was originally known as the Green Man and doubtless the change of name was due to confusion with the Old Green Man in Bromford Lane. The hotel had a reputation for considerable disturbances during the annual Wakes and in 1815 it temporarily lost its licence.

On the right of this view of the Chester Road and Kingsbury Road junctions is Tyburn House. The photograph was taken on 14 February 1934, four years after the new Tyburn was built. The Cotswold-type design came from the architects Bateman and Bateman who created it for the brewers, Ansells. It is still one of the best-known landmarks on the Chester Road.

The original three-storey Tyburn House, famous for its connections with the Mary Ashford murder case in 1819. Here photographed by the local photographer Sir Benjamin Stone in 1893, and looking suitably forbidding.

The Vesey Club paying a visit to the Old Green Man in Bromford Lane on 21 October 1911. The plaque on the left of the photograph bears the legend 'Known as the Lad in the Lane, Established 1306'. It is claimed to be the ninth oldest pub in the country. Basically the building is of fourteenth-century origin but only some of the beams are of that date as it was altered and enlarged extensively in the thirties. It is a grade -2 listed building.

STOCKLAND GREEN FROM RESERVOIR ROAD.

The newly-built Stockland Hotel as it was then called in this twenties' postcard view taken from Reservoir Road. A recognisable but much altered scene now with the bushes and the trees, the trams and the man with a cart have long departed. The large building on the right is the Fondella café.

Above and below: A book produced by Mitchells and Butlers in 1928 eulogised the newly-built pubs on the outskirts of the city such as the Stockland, the Antelope at Sparkhill and The Yew Tree at Yardley. The pubs were set back from the road so 'the patrons are not expected to slink furtively up to the entrances; many will drive in their cars or on their motorcycles and have no more compunction about entering these portals than they would about entering a hotel in town'. Gardens were another special feature of the new Mitchells and Butlers inns. To quote, 'These houses also have their pleasure gardens which are an integral part of the scheme of improvement. But they are not the old-fashioned tea-gardens of the last century. Gone are the insect-haunted bowers. The gardens of Mitchells and Butlers houses are open and formal in style, laid out with broad flagged walks, between wide flower beds or close clipped hedges and with large bowling greens which are true enough to satisfy the most fastidious bowler'. Sadly the current state of the gardens at the Stockland rather mocks this pretence.

A splendid postcard view of the Red Lion at the Station Road/Short Heath Road junction. The present building which was constructed for Mitchells and Butlers in 1899 was built on the site of an earlier Victorian pub. It was designed by the architects Wood and Kenrick and is a brick building with horizontal bands of stone, a really fine feature. (Andrew Maxam)

A view of the Red Lion with its clock tower looking down Short Heath Road, taken in March 1959.

The Red Lion is splendid inside as well. The bar front shown here has a beautiful array of ceramic tiles almost certainly made by the firm of Craven Dunnill. Unlike the Gunmakers in Lozells for example where the whole bar front was stolen, the pub interior has remained virtually unchanged over the last century.

Across the Short Heath Road from the Red Lion, the Royal Oak provides a contrast in styles. In this postcard view from 1959 the street appears deserted and the pub closed. Although much smaller than the Royal Oak, and at times threatened with demolition for road widening, it has survived and still supports a regular clientele. An article on Erdington pubs in 1913 has a nice description of the Red Lion. The landlord was the genial Tom Fiddian – the famous old Birchfield Harrier. Apparently 'connoisseurs of malt liquor aver that you get the best glass of beer at the 'Oak' and certainly the number of jugs and bottles that are filled daily at the bar for home consumption affords evidence of the truth of this contention of the man in the street'. (Andrew Maxam)

Within a stone's throw of the Red Lion and the Royal Oak was, and still is, the New Inns in Summer Road. A Victorian pub, the Three Tuns was the predecessor to the New Inns. It is probable that the change of name occurred when the Three Tuns was rebuilt at the end of the nineteenth century. (Andrew Maxam)

The Brookvale on Slade Road. It was built in 1934 on the site of several mid-nineteenth-century houses next to the Star cinema. (Andrew Maxam)

The Navigation on the corner of Bromford Lane and Tyburn Road in December 1972. Like many Erdington pubs, the present building was not the original inn. The earlier pub was just beyond the canal bridge while the new Navigation was built on this site in about 1930.

One of Erdington's newest pubs, the Leopard in Jerry's Lane, seen here on 5 September 1961. The pub was built around 1939.

The gateway and entrance drive to The Digby pub on the Chester Road, 2 April 1957. At this date it was still a club rather than a pub hence the sign, now gone, and the distance from the road.

The Queens Head at the Six Ways on 18 October 1955. Again this is not the original building on the site, which was a fairly small Victorian coaching inn. This was pulled down in the thirties and the present building erected further back from the main road. The pub, which looks very splendid here, is now sadly derelict and awaiting demolition.

The off-licence on the corner of Summer Road and Gravelly Lane. The building is now a photographer's studio, while the garage to the right is a garden centre.

The Erdington Arms, which fell victim to the construction of Spaghetti Junction and was replaced by the very different-looking Armada. (Andrew Maxam)

An early postcard view of the Cross Keys pub on the corner of Station Road and the High Street.

The Bagot, photographed on 10 March 1985.

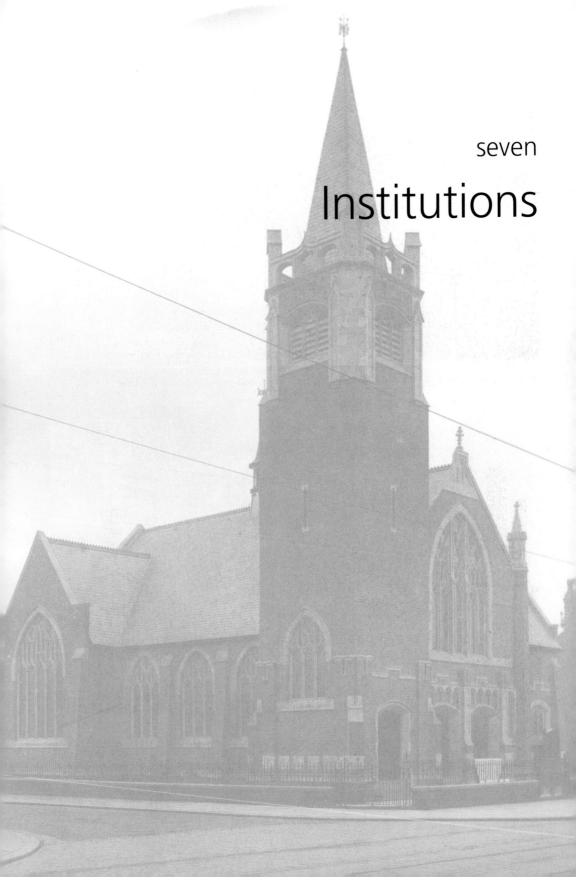

seven

Institutions

The Erdington Cottage Homes. The architects were Franklin, Cross and Nichols and the building was commissioned by the Aston Board of Guardians and built at a cost of 363,000. The foundation stone was laid on 26 July 1898. The builders were Messrs Lee & Sons of Avenue Road, Aston.

W.J. Adams presented the clock to the Guardians of the Cottage Homes. Member of the Aston Board of Guardians where he was a great advocate of the betterment of children, and a prime mover in the building of the Cottage Homes.

Miss Sherlock pouring tea for some of the children at the Cottage Homes. One man's recollection of time at the Cottage Homes in the 1930s is given by Bob Mackenzie in an article in the *Birmingham Historian*, issue number 15. One story told in the article paints a vivid picture of the way in which boys from the Cottage Homes were regarded at that time. At the annual school exams at Slade Road School the head announced that the top boy was Bob Mackenzie. He then announced 'I am surprised you let a Cottage boy beat you all.'

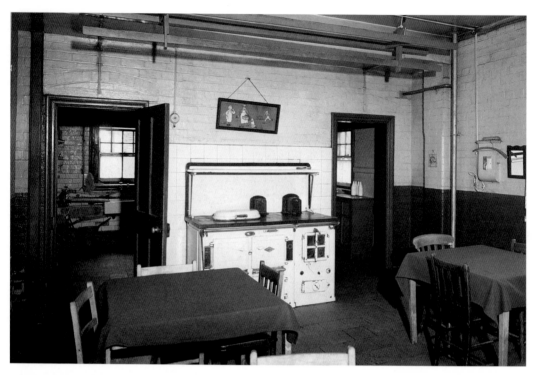

Above and below: Two views of the dining rooms at the Cottage Homes. These and subsequent interior photographs have come from the City's Architects Department and were taken in around 1952 to illustrate before and after renovation. The top photograph is 'before'.

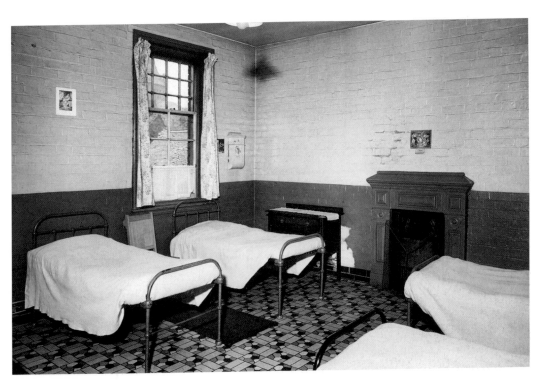

Above and below: Typical bedrooms at the Cottage Homes. Again the top photograph is taken before the renovation.

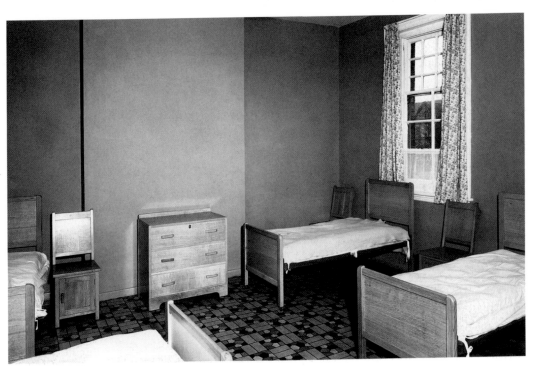

The kitchens. Not too difficult to spot the new windows and the replacement for the 'Belfast' sink – now likely to be restored in many a trendy domestic kitchen.

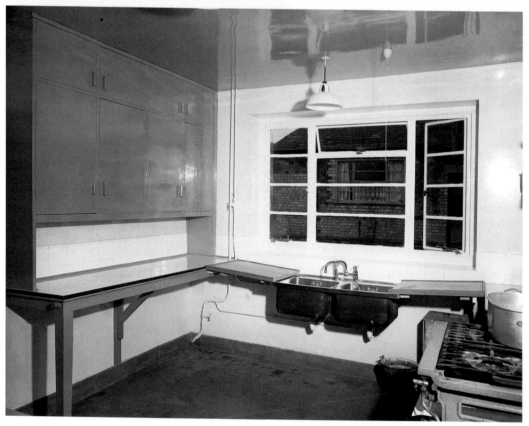

The Workhouse was built in the 1860s for the Aston Manor Board of Guardians to accommodate the feeble and aged people on the Aston side of Birmingham. For many years it was known as Erdington House, but changed its name in 1942 to Highcroft Hall because, as the official explanation put it, 'the character of the residents had changed and it was no longer appropriate to call it a workhouse'.

An aerial view of Erdington House taken during a visit by members of the Public Assistance Committee in 1931. It was later renamed Highcroft Hall. In July 1948 it was taken over by the government and became a mental hospital. Its present fate is not secure because since the hospital has closed many of its buildings have been vandalised and work has yet to start on the proposed conversion to residential accommodation. The main building and the front entrance range both opened in 1869 and were designed by Yeoville Thomason, having grade-2 listed status.

Above and below: Erdington Six Ways Baptist church. The lower view was taken in September 1959. The church, a familiar landmark at the Six Ways, was subsequently demolished for new shops and a replacement church built just round the corner in Wood End Road.

Above and below: Postcard views of the exterior and interior of Erdington Parish church, St Barnabas.

Pype Hayes Congregational church on the Chester Road, opposite the park. The photograph is taken from the front cover of the programme for the opening ceremony for the church which took place on Saturday July 12 1930.

Erdington Congregational church. An early writer on the churches of Erdington gave the following description of the building: 'Erdington chapel is one of the few which possess a 'God's acre' and the association of grass-grown graves. It stands well back from the road; in the summertime it is half hidden by trees and you walk up to it through an avenue lined by mossy tombstones. Its architecture though unpretending is also inoffensive. It's true that it is only built of brick but it is rather pretty otherwise'.

Above and below: St Thomas Abbey and its extensive and rustic grounds. The photograph of the grounds, in fact the orchard, was taken in around 1918 and the Abbey tower can be seen in the distance.

The High Street Methodist church at the corner of Newman Road. The church was built before the First World War through the efforts of the Revd Harvey Roe, who became its first Minister. It was constructed to replace an iron hut on the same site. In 1955 a large church hall was built at the rear, but the church and hall were demolished in 1971.

Slade Assembly Hall in Hunton Road was built around 1925 and was a Plymouth Brethren chapel.

A postcard view of the Original Mission Church of St Marks, Stockland Road. The small brick building with a slated roof comprised a main hall, side rooms, bellcot and one bell which was rung from within. It had various names and guises being an un-denominational church originally after it opened in 1886. Subsequently acquired by the Methodists, it was then sold to the Church of England in 1906 before being demolished and houses built on the site.

The small building on the right in Edwards Road is being used as wholesale stationers in 1976. It is currently used as a spiritualist place of worship.

Erdington Conservative Club at 93 Orphanage Road. The building was used for many years as a convent school before being acquired by the Erdington Conservative Club for a club house in 1909. The bowling green attached to the club had the reputation of being the finest in the Midlands and is still well used today.

eight

Around the
High Street

Sutton New Road looking north from Six Ways before alterations, July 1937.

Sutton New Road looking north from Reservoir Road after alterations have been completed, May 1939. According to an article in a Birmingham newspaper of 1938, the roundabout traffic island at Six Ways was not only the first to be erected in Birmingham but the first in the country.

A view of Erdington High Street taken outside the Acorn Hotel, looking towards Six Ways, 1954. York Road is on the right.

Coton Lane is seen here on the left with Newman Lane opposite; Wrenson's is on the corner, 1955. Wrenson's was due to close down and re-open on the opposite side of the road. Note the tall trees around the parish churchyard.

Looking towards Barnabas Road, with the Parish church on the right. Church House is on the left, beyond Dolcis shoe shop. One of the compilers remembers having many shoes bought by her mother from this shop. Above the sixth car on the left are small shops, which were created from old Easy Row. They were demolished around 1963. This postcard is dated 1954.

Woolworth and Company Limited, on the corner of High Street and Barnabas Road, March 1961.

Advertisement taken from Saxton's Monthly Recorder, 1911.

Seen here on the left in 1955, The Palace Theatre was built as the Public Hall and opened as a cinema on 26 December 1912. Chas Miller's hairdressing establishment just beyond, was anciently the White Lion Inn; and later served as the Post Office; then the fire station (a bell having been hung from the chimney); and finally as a shop. It was taken down in 1958.

View looking towards Coton Lane, which is on the left in the distance, *c.* 1954. Holway's Post Office, which is on the left of this view, was transferred to Wood End Road. The block of shops nearest the camera and defined by the lower roofs were taken down in around 1963.

The advertisement on the Palace cinema reads 'The House of the perfect pictures and Western Electric'. The greengrocers are next door. The row of old houses and shops next to the milk float were taken down around 1933. Note the outside displays of Fosters, Coulbourn's and Perkins, when the pavements were not so crowded. Benton's then had a public telephone. Dick's Grill Room is on the left and the passage to the left of Perkins' lead to gardens at the rear. This view is from around 1919.

Looking towards the Village Green on a busy Saturday, *c.* 1948.

Advertisement from Saxton's Monthly Recorder, 1912.

High Street, April 1929. In 1938 Sutton New Road was completed and much of the traffic was diverted from the High Street along the new road, including the trams, which had had to operate on a single track through the narrow part of the High Street.

The old railings have gone from the Green. The Picture House and Wilson's chemist is on the left, *c.* 1947.

High Street, *c.* 1935. The trams have been routed along the new road, so this view was taken after 1934. The old lamp is situated over the Jubilee stone. The new Britannic Insurance office is on the corner. A four-mile stone was set in the wall of Dean's Drapery shop before the Britannic was rebuilt in 1933. Philip Newman's photographic establishment was above Leah Taylor's gown shop, which stands on the site of John Wilton's butcher shop and bears the inscription 'J.W. Estab. 1794' – the date John Wilton opened his shop.

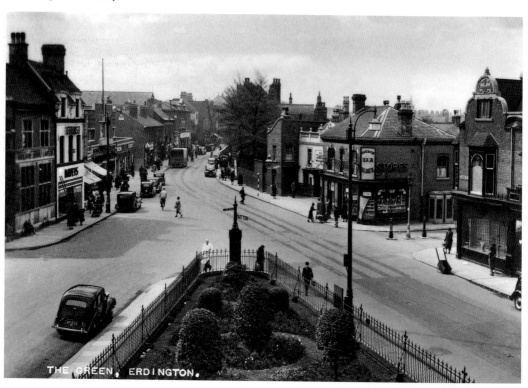

Looking to the High Street from the Village Green, *c.* 1954. This view shows the Village Green before it was turfed over. Mason Road is on the left. Note the unaltered façade of the Swan Inn, with its eighteenth-century wing on the left, and Shuffle Brothers Provision Stores on the right. The large tree has gone from the grounds of the Swan Inn and the Picture House is now adjacent.

Right: The title page of the official programme for the opening of the new Erdington swimming baths, 6 May 1925.

Opposite below: The Village Green looking down the High Street, *c.* 1938. The tramlines have been roughly covered but the Midland Red timetable is still on the railings. The tree in the centre right is in the gardens of the Swan Inn, and the directional post is still on the Jubilee stone.

CITY OF BIRMINGHAM.

BATHS DEPARTMENT.

Official Opening of New Public Baths
Mason Road, Erdington
by ALDERMAN T. O. WILLIAMS, J.P.

Above: Numbers 32-38 High Street, August 1951. Originally called 'Bell Villas' in Bell Lane, Bell Lane being the old name for Orphanage Road. A plan of 1815 was drawn up to indicate possible sites for the new parish church and this is the first time Belle Villas are mentioned, being alongside the earlier built houses of numbers 24 and 26.

Opposite above: The entrance to Erdington swimming baths. When first opened the building was made up of washing bath suites for men and women and a Turkish bath suite only. The Turkish baths are comprised of three hot rooms, a steam room (Russian bath), a plunge pool, a cooling room/rest room, a needle shower and a shampoo room.

Opposite below: The pool at Erdington swimming baths. An aerate bath was added to the building on 21 November 1955 at a cost of £299 15s 6d. This bath is circular in shape and is constructed in stainless steel. Designed to be used by one person at a time, the treatment lasts for fifteen to twenty minutes and produces a warm hydraulic massage in a weightless condition. This is achieved by using 230 gallons of water heated to body temperature in conjunction with 75 cubic feet per minute of air being directed upwards and downwards. The air bubbles are vibrated as they pass the body.

Numbers 24 and 26 High Street. Now set well back from the road these two houses are shown on a map of 1760 when they stood on the grass verge. In around 1812 the road width was standardised when the new turnpike was opened, leaving the cottages at their apparently odd angle.

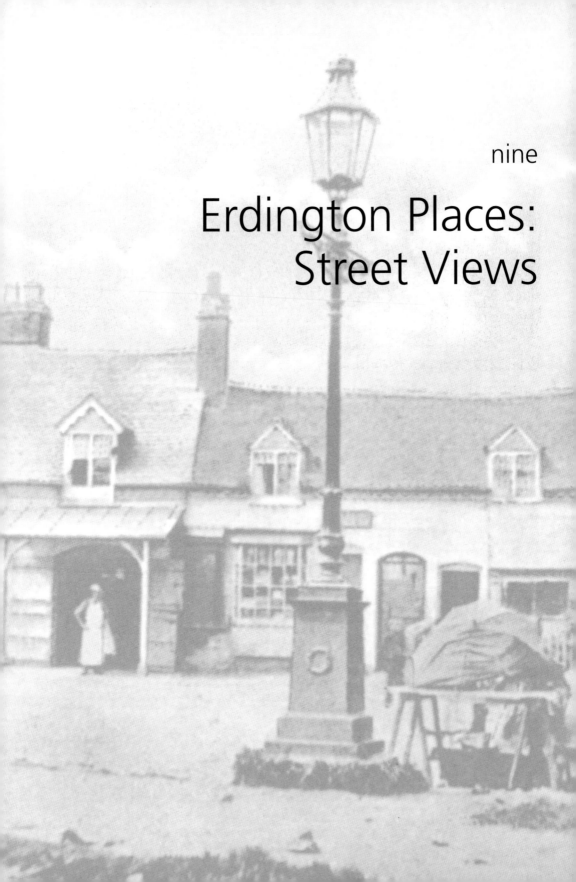

nine

Erdington Places:
Street Views

Above and below: A bygone age: Leaholme House on the Short Heath Road. The house, which was built in 1894, is surprisingly still there. In recent years the building has been used as a residential home for old people but this has since closed and the building is currently empty and looking rather forlorn.

The wide open spaces of Short Heath Road in November 1934. This photograph was taken by a police photographer for use as evidence in a road accident case.

Cottages on Wood End Lane in August 1982 – still some of the most desirable residences in Erdington.

Marsh Lane on 10 December 1858, showing Barnes' fish and chip shop at number 4 and the Paragon laundry. There had been a chippie at this address since the end of the nineteenth century.

The junction of Marsh Hill and Gipsy Lane in 1925. Notice the condition of the road – it would be another year before the outer circle buses would be passing here.

Numbers 44–50 Gravelly Lane on 28 November 1960, when it was presumably still safe to leave bicycles unlocked outside your house.

Shops on Gravelly Lane on June 4 1926. The shops are still there today, although Gravelly Lane is no longer the major shopping centre it was in 1926.

The destruction of a row of houses in Milverton Road after a bomb landed in a back garden.

The results of heavy rain at Wylde Green railway bridge in September 1950.

Station Road looking down towards the station bridge, 25 November 1952. The cottages on the left were subsequently demolished, an all too familiar story in Erdington, to make way for Osborne nursery school. The coal merchants at number 14, Walkers, is offering six bags of logs for twenty-one shillings.

Another bridge on the cross-city line, this time at Slade Road on 12 August 1955, looking towards Gravelly Hill.

The Kingsbury Road and Tyburn Road junction, around 1932. The same view after the construction of the island where the horse and cart are in this photograph appeared in the earlier volume by the same authors (*Erdington*, page 97). The cart is advertising Wright's Grade-A milk. A new central reservation is being constructed in Holly Lane.

A postcard view of the High Street from around 1919, showing Station and Edwards Road junction. The large building on the right is the premises of Prices' Removals, next door to the Cross Keys.

Above: Taken on 13 March 1957 this photograph shows the now-demolished cottage at number 37 Sutton Road.

Left: Erdington Village Green in around 1875.

Opposite bottom: The old cottages on the Chester Road close to the Yenton on 13 October 1938. Too much of Erdington's heritage has gone the same way as these cottages.

Above: A very attractive postcard of part of Silverbirch Road, with the spire of Josiah Mason's orphanage in the distance.

Above: A charming view of Church Road looking away from the High Street.

Left: A publicity shot encouraging prospective homebuyers to move to Erdington.